Raising Babies

What Animal Parents Do

Dona Herweck Rice

Consultants

Sally Creel, Ed.D.
Curriculum Consultant

Leann Iacuone, M.A.T., NBCT, ATC
Riverside Unified School District

Jill Tobin
California Teacher of the Year
Semi-Finalist
Burbank Unified School District

Image Credits: Cover & p.1 Juniors Bildarchiv GmbH/Alamy; p.19 John Daniels/ardea/age fotostock; p.14 Blickwinkel/Alamy; p.2 Roy Toft/ National Geographic Creative; pp.20–21 (illustrations) Janelle Bell-Martin; all other images from Shutterstock.

Library of Congress Cataloging-in-Publication Data

Rice, Dona, author.
Raising babies: what animal parents do / Dona Herweck Rice; consultants Sally Creel, Ed.D. curriculum consultant, Leann Iacuone, M.A.T., NBCT, ATC Riverside Unified School District, Jill Tobin, California Teacher of the Year Semi-Finalist Burbank Unified School District.
pages cm
Includes index.
ISBN 978-1-4807-4561-2 (pbk.)
ISBN 978-1-4807-5051-7 (ebook)
1. Parental behavior in animals—Juvenile literature.
2. Animals—Infancy—Juvenile literature. I. Title.
QL762.R53 2015
591.56´3—dc23

2014013144

Teacher Created Materials
5301 Oceanus Drive
Huntington Beach, CA 92649-1030
http://www.tcmpub.com

ISBN 978-1-4807-4561-2

Printed by: 590835
Printed in: China

Table of Contents

Being a Parent

It takes a lot to **raise** a baby! That is true for people. It is true for other animals, too.

This woman cares for her new baby.

This kangaroo is a new parent.

How do animals raise their **young**? Each animal has its own way.

Oh, Baby!

How do people care for their babies? How do other animals care for their babies? Is it the same?

A penguin feeds its chick.

A polar bear
bathes its cub.

Caring for Baby

Some animals raise their young for a short while. They may leave just after the baby is born.

But elephants raise their young for a long time. They get help, too. They find babysitters in their **herd** to help them.

Many animals keep their young safe. Rhinos (RAHY-nohs) are **fierce**! They may fight a lion to save their baby.

Hold On!

A mother orangutan (aw-RANG-oo-tan) holds her baby for its first few months of life.

This rhino keeps its baby safe.

Some animals play with their young. Play keeps the babies strong. Mother pandas roll around with their young.

A mother panda plays with her cub.

This lion cub grows strong by playing with its mother.

Some animals teach their young how to act. A wolf **nips** at its pup when it does what it should not. The wolf grabs the pup with its teeth to carry it away.

In It Together

Whole **colonies** of ants work together to feed and take care of their young.

Ants bring food back to their home to feed younger ants.

Some animals name their babies! They make a sound for the name. Dolphins do this.

A parrot may change its name when it is grown. It may make the name longer. It may make the name shorter. That is like a **nickname**!

A parrot takes care of its baby.

Let's Do Science!

How do animals carry their young? Try this and see!

What to Get

- paper and pencil
- pictures of animal parents and their babies

What to Do

1. Find at least six pictures of animal parents carrying their babies.

2. Make a chart like this one. List the animals on the left. List how they carry their babies on the right.

Animal	How it carries its babies
kangaroo	in pouch

3. Look at your chart. What do you see? Do some animals carry their babies in the same ways as others? Do any of them carry their babies in different ways?

Glossary

colonies—groups of animals living in the same places

fierce—angry and wild

herd—a group of one kind of animal

nickname—a name used in place of a real name

nips—gently bites

raise—take care of young until it is grown up

young—children

Index

Your Turn!

The World Around You

Look for animal parents and babies in the world around you. What do you see? What are they doing? Draw a picture of an animal parent you see caring for its baby.